Kent

Janet Cameron

COUNTRYSIDE BOOKS
NEWBURY BERKSHIRE

First Published 2006
© Janet Cameron, 2006

All rights reserved. No reproduction
permitted without the prior permission
of the publisher:

COUNTRYSIDE BOOKS
3 Catherine Road
Newbury, Berkshire

To view our complete range of books,
please visit us at
www.countrysidebooks.co.uk

ISBN 1 85306 979 5
EAN 978 1 85306 979 6

Cover picture of Chilham by David Sellman

Photographs and maps by Philip Howdle
Designed by Peter Davies, Nautilus Design
Produced through MRM Associates Ltd, Reading
Printed by Woolnough Bookbinding Ltd., Irthlingborough

Contents

Area map showing location of the walks

Introduction

The fifteen walks in this book are specially chosen for you to enjoy all the infinite variety of landscapes to be found in Kent, justifiably called the Garden of England. I have included routes that are not so well known outside their immediate locality, so I hope you will find something new here to intrigue you.

There are traditional English country walks through woodlands, meadows, farmland and orchards as well as lovely marshland, coastal, estuary and riverside strolls, all rich in bird and plant life. All the routes are circular, using designated footpaths and country lanes, and range from 2 miles (1 or 1½ miles if you decide to do only one part of the Conyer Creek walk) to 5 miles long. Points of interest are detailed to enhance your enjoyment.

The pubs have been chosen for their good food and friendly service (and, of course, the beer). All the landlords are happy for patrons to use their parking facilities while they are walking, but it would be appreciated if you would ask first, and telephone in advance if you are walking as a group.

Sketch maps are included to give you an overview of the circuit to be followed. It is always a good idea, though, to take with you the relevant Ordnance Survey map as well. This will help you identify the main features and views. An indication of the terrain for each walk is given and it is worth remembering that those routes which include hills will often reward you with especially fine vistas of glorious, unspoilt countryside once you have reached the top.

Although the walks are on footpaths and along quiet country lanes, there are some instances where it is necessary to follow roads for a short distance either to gain access to a circuit or to link one part of a route to another. Do look and listen carefully for approaching traffic on these sections. Finally, the correct footwear is essential – some paths can become wet and slippery after rain so it is worth being well shod.

I hope you will gain as much enjoyment in experiencing all the walks in this book as I have in preparing them and wish you a happy, healthy time discovering the many delights of Kent's rich heritage.

Garret Cameron

Acknowledgements

Thanks to Rachel and Gareth Cameron, and to Edwina and Geoff Pegg for helping test the walks and to Ben Latter for kindly sharing his computer graphics skills. Also to my editor, Paula Leigh, for support and advice.

Publisher's Note

We hope that you obtain considerable enjoyment from this book; great care has been taken in its preparation. However, changes of landlord and actual closures are sadly not uncommon. Likewise, although at the time of publication all routes followed public rights of way or permitted paths, diversion orders can be made and permissions withdrawn.

We cannot, of course, be held responsible for such diversion orders and any inaccuracies in the text which result from these or any other changes to the routes nor any damage which might result from walkers trespassing on private property. We are anxious though that all details covering the walks and pubs are kept up to date and would therefore welcome information from readers which would be relevant to future editions.

The simple sketch maps that accompany the walks in this book are based on notes made by the author whilst checking out the routes on the ground. However, for the benefit of a proper map, we do recommend that you purchase the relevant Ordnance Survey sheet covering your walk. The Ordnance Survey maps are widely available, especially through booksellers and local newsagents.

1 Hildenborough

The Plough

This easy, flattish walk along comfortable footpaths passes through open countryside, woodlands, by a lake and along a quiet part of the River Medway, where willows are reflected in the still waters. Meadows bursting with wild flowers for much of the year are a botanist's dream! Early on in the circuit you will be travelling along a quiet country lane, Powder Mills, which takes its name from the site of mills where gunpowder was produced from around 1812 until the early 20th century.

THE PUB The **Plough**, set back from the road, is a quaint 16th-century pub, once a row of labourer's cottages and smithy, which was renovated in the 1970s. Festooned with hanging baskets in the summer, it is a delightful, welcoming

Distance – 2 miles.

OS Explorer 147 Sevenoaks and Tonbridge. GR 567468

Flattish, easy walking, mostly on well-trodden paths.

Starting point The Plough in Leigh Road, Hildenborough.

How to get there Hildenborough is on the B245 approximately 2 miles north-west of the centre of Tonbridge. The Plough is reached by turning south off the B2027 to the south of Hildenborough and continuing along Leigh Road. Patrons may leave their cars in the pub car park while walking (please ask first). Alternatively, on street parking is available near point 2 of the walk.

establishment. Inside, adding to the cosiness, there are beamed ceilings, wood-blocked floors and old oak tables at which you can enjoy a delicious home-cooked meal. You can choose traditional food, for example the chef's home-made pies, or you can opt for a wonderful 'Tagliatelle Alfredo' with bacon, garlic bread and salad. Adjoining is the 'great barn' where you can order a Sunday roast in the Carvery. The beers are Harvey's Best, Spitfire and Adnams. Outside is a large beer garden.

Opening hours: 12 noon to 3 pm and 6 pm to 11 pm on Tuesday to Saturday (closed Mondays) and 12 noon to 5 pm on Sundays. Food is served from 12 noon to 2.30 pm and 6 pm to 9.30 pm on Tuesday to Saturday. On Sunday the main menu and Carvery is available from 12 noon to 2.30 pm and snacks until 4.30 pm.
☎ *01732 832149*

Hildenborough Walk 1

1 Turn left out of the pub and walk up the country lane, watching for occasional traffic as there is no footpath. Shortly, turn right into a lane named **Powder Mills**, noting the converted oast house on the corner. Continue along the lane, crossing a bridge and at the T-junction, turn left down **Hunter Seal**.

2 Go left again along the footpath, so the backs of the houses are on your right and farmland is on your left. Soon houses are replaced by woodlands. As you cross the stone bridge, you will see a lake to your left. Follow the footpath until it bears to the right, away from the lake. Cross a stone bridge and then take the right fork signposted to **Haysden Country Park**.

3 Continue along this footpath, cross another stone bridge, and a few yards on, yet another stone bridge. Keep to the path along the riverbank on your left, with fields to your right. Look

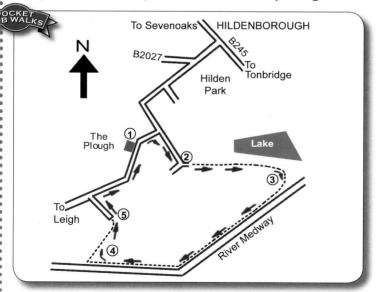

Kent

out on your right for the remains of Second World War fortifications. Ignore a further footbridge on your left. (This leads to **Haysden Country Park**, which you might like to visit another time.) After passing another footbridge on your left, you'll reach a metal farm gate, with a weir ahead. Do not pass through this gate.

The River Medway.

4 The walk veers diagonally to the right, along a footpath crossing the meadow. You should be able to spot the signposted marker at the other end. Go to the right of the signpost and down a set of steps, over a stone bridge and up again. Continue straight ahead across the meadow, bearing slightly left towards another signpost with a wooden pylon close by.

5 Keep to the right of the post and pylon, making for a wide grass track (a small stream runs under the track). Go up the track to a metal gate and climb the stile on the left. Continue along the track, to the right (there is a farm entrance on the left) until you reach **Leigh Road**. Turn right and continue along the country lane to return to the **Plough** on your left.

Places of interest nearby

Tonbridge Castle is just off the main High Street in the centre of Tonbridge, with car parks nearby. This is a fascinating 13th-century 'motte and bailey' castle with audio tours to help you discover life in medieval times.
☎ *01732 770929*

2 Stansted

The Black Horse

This is a wonderful, tranquil walk, across pasture and through delightful wooded paths and lanes. The village of Stansted offers lovely views northwards towards Gravesend and the Thames Estuary and southwards towards the Weald of Kent. The old church of St Mary the Virgin, dating from the 13th century, is a short distance from the pub and boasts a yew tree dating from the 18th century in its churchyard. The pub is set on one of the highest points of the Downs so the walk includes some hills, but your efforts are amply rewarded by being constantly surrounded by a glorious panorama.

Kent

THE PUB The **Black Horse** is a lovely, lively pub with a distinctly Irish tradition (and live Irish music in the bar sometimes at lunchtime on Sunday). The menu includes dishes such as crispy chicken fillet strips and an 8oz gammon steak with tomatoes, mushrooms and fried egg. Or perhaps you'd prefer curry, chilli or a jacket potato. There are also vegetarian options. A roast meal is offered on Sundays. The real ales served in this free house include the best-selling Larkins Traditional, Westerham Brewery's 7X and Welton's Old Cocky bitter.

Opening hours are 11 am to 11 pm. Food is served 12 noon to 3 pm (4 pm on Sundays).
☎ *01732 822355*

Distance – 2½ miles.

OS Explorer 148 Maidstone and the Medway Towns or 147 Sevenoaks and Tonbridge GR 606618

Downland ups and downs; be prepared for frequent stiles.

Starting point The Black Horse in Tumblefield Road, Stansted.

How to get there *Stansted village is one mile off the A20 north of Wrotham. Turn off the A20 at West Kingsdown into Stansted Lane. If approaching on the M20, leave it at junction 2. Customers may leave their cars in the car park of the Black Horse whilst walking, but please ring in advance.*

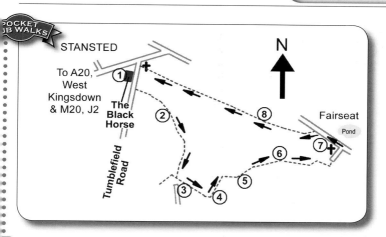

1 Turn right from the **Black Horse**. After approximately 200 yards, take a public footpath signposted left along a track. Climb the stile ahead and cross a field with a hedgerow to your right, then climb another stile, signposted, bearing right. Follow a footpath downhill and descend steps through a copse. Shortly, climb a stile into a field, signposted and bearing diagonally right towards another stile. Climb the stile.

2 Continue uphill, bearing right, signposted. Climb the next stile, signposted through woods and follow the footpath with a wire fence to your left. Soon climb another stile and follow the continuation of the footpath. At the end of the path, climb a stile into a field. Cross the field diagonally left and climb the stile by the greenhouse.

3 Follow the footpath curving left, with a fence to your right, past a house. Pass a redundant stile, signposted ahead. Shortly, pass another redundant stile, signposted right, and bear right onto the continuation of the footpath, downhill. Enter a copse and climb the stile. Continue slightly left, uphill, towards a metal gate. Do not pass through the gate.

St Mary's church.

4 Turn left, taking a footpath alongside the perimeter of the fence, now on your right. Shortly, take a right fork in the path and climb the stile, signposted, entering woods and bearing left along a footpath uphill. The way is shown by yellow markers on trees. Follow this winding footpath to the fenced edge of a field. Continue in the same direction, with the fence on your right.

5 Shortly, the path curves left and away from the field into woods, descending, and signposted on trees. At the end, climb a stile into a field, signposted ahead. Continue with the fence and woods on your left for about 30 yards, then cross the field downhill to the stile ahead. Climb the stile and immediately climb another stile, both stiles allowing passage through fences.

6 Follow the footpath ahead and go through a metal gate signposted ahead, passing a hillock on your right. Climb a stone-stepped stile ahead beside a gate and turn left. Walk two sides of the field's perimeter. At the end of the second side, take the second farm gate on your left, signposted on the fence, and pass between wooden fences, going through another metal gate and farm buildings towards houses.

7 At the church on the corner, opposite the village pond in **Fairseat**, turn left into the lane. Take great care on the bend in the lane, watching and listening for traffic. After a few yards, follow the public footpath signposted left and climb the stile into a field. Cross the field to go over the stile opposite. Follow a footpath across the next field, bearing slightly left towards a single tall tree standing in the hedgerow. As you face the tree, turn right and continue with the hedgerow on your left.

8 Soon, take a footpath to your left through a copse, then climb a stile into a field. Bear right, downhill, towards **St Mary's church**, along the footpath to a kissing gate in the hedgerow. Continue bearing right towards the church and climb a stile, signposted, between two metal gates. Go through a kissing gate into the churchyard and follow the footpath to the church entrance, exiting opposite the **Black Horse**.

Places of interest nearby

Eagle Heights Bird of Prey Centre is at Lullingstone Lane, Eynsford, to the north-west of Stansted, off the A225. Enjoy seeing eagles, hawks, falcons and vultures up close as well as a fine reptile collection. There are regular outdoor displays and a café/tearoom.
☎ *01322 866466*

The Copperfield

This green and peaceful stroll meanders through the rolling English countryside beloved by poets and artists, and you can enjoy both traditional woodland and glorious open meadows with grazing horses. Be sure to look over your shoulder to appreciate the gradually unfolding vista of the River Thames in the distance. The circuit takes you along Shorne Ridgeway and through the village of Shorne itself, with its long and fascinating history. An archaeological dig in 1957 revealed the foundations of a small Norman church there. During the 19th century, an enterprising builder, Tufnell Carbonell Barrett, reclaimed an area of bogland on the eastern side of the village, turning it into fertile land for farming and on which he built some quaint Elizabethan-style cottages.

Distance – 3 miles.

OS Explorer 163 Gravesend and Rochester. GR 695717

Easy walking on gentle, undulating hills.

Starting point The Copperfield in Shorne.

How to get there *The Copperfield is just under 3 miles from the town of Gravesend and located on the A226 (Gravesend Road). Customers may leave their cars in the pub car park while walking. Alternatively, park in the lay-by on the main road as you approach Higham.*

THE PUB

The **Copperfield** is a roomy, well-run, fairly modern Whitbread pub, which welcomes families with children. It offers a varied Brewer's Fayre menu comprising everyone's favourite pub food, including sausage 'n' mash in a giant Yorkshire pudding, steak, mushroom and ale pie, and a vegetable lasagne. There's a selection of breakfasts, grills and lighter dishes as well as appetizing desserts, such as caramel apple betty, cheesecake or profiteroles. Yummy! Tetley Extra Smooth bitter is served, alongside a good selection of lagers and wines. Outside there is a beer garden as well as a raised terrace.

Opening hours: 11 am to 11 pm on Monday to Saturday and 12 noon to 10.30 pm on Sunday. Food is served from 11.30 am to 10 pm on Monday to Saturday and 12 noon to 9.30 pm on Sunday.
☎ *01474 822395*

On leaving the **Copperfield**, turn left and walk along the pavement to the third traffic island, at which point you carefully cross the

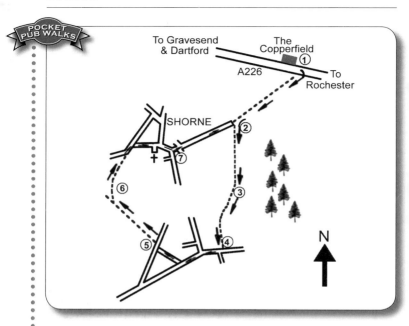

A226. Once safely on the other side, turn right and backtrack a few yards, then take the signposted footpath (now on your left) into the field. Go straight across the field, following the footpath. Remember to look, not only at the glorious countryside ahead, but back at views over the **River Thames**. After crossing the field, enter woodland and immediately bear left.

2 Descend steps where you will find an intersection of footpaths. Ignore the right turn. Go ahead, joining a track that runs along the left side of a treeline. On reaching the farm gate ahead of you, enjoy the peaceful, pastoral scene. You may spot Muffin the Donkey in the meadow ahead, among the horses. Muffin is a clever, mischievous donkey and very good at escaping! However, he does go to church in Shorne village once a year, on Palm Sunday, so he can't be all bad!

3 After looking over the farm gate, skirt the hedgerow on your right, bearing left around it. Take the left fork of the footpath alongside the same field, now to your left. Continue through meadows, slightly uphill. Soon, enter a copse and immediately climb old steps and go along the footpath ahead, skirting woods to your left with wooden palings on your right. Climb a stile into a field, keeping to the right alongside hedgerows. Farm buildings are to your right and a row of bungalows to your left. Climb the stile into **Pear Tree Lane** opposite a pub called the **See Ho**.

4 Turn right along **Pear Tree Lane**, still enjoying views over the countryside you've just walked. As this lane becomes **The Ridgeway**, ignore the first signposted footpath to your right to **Ifield and Thong**. Take the second, wide public footpath right, by **Hanbury Cottages**. At the end of the footpath, turn right along the minor road, watching for traffic.

Muffin the Donkey, a Shorne celebrity!

Kent

5 After a few yards cross the road carefully and take the footpath to your left, adjacent to a white house. Follow this downhill path between gardens till you reach a kissing gate. Pass through and go straight ahead, across the meadow, to climb the stile on the far side.

6 Turn right, waymarked through the woods, to **Shorne Hill**. Continue to some wider open spaces between trees. Go ahead to a level footpath running along the left side of a large copsed mound. Shortly, turn right into **Mill Hill Lane**, watching for traffic, then, after few yards, take a right-hand fork along **Butcher's Hill**, passing between two bollards. At the next set of bollards, ignore the cul-de-sac to a church on your right. Continue ahead and cross the road carefully, passing between **The Old Vicarage** and the **Rose and Crown** pub. Shortly, turn left at **Swillars Lane**.

7 Continue along **Swillars Lane** until you reach a footpath ahead. Go straight on, ignoring a fork to the right. Ignore another fork to the right, keeping straight ahead to the first field you crossed at the beginning of the walk. Retrace your steps across this field, climb the stile and exit onto the A226. It would be safest to turn right, walk a few paces and cross at the traffic island. Then turn left and make your way back to the pub. You have now completed a beautiful, traditional English country walk.

Places of interest nearby

The keep of **Rochester Castle** is one of the tallest in the country. Located in Rochester town centre, the castle is open daily except Christmas Day, 10 am to 4 pm in winter and 10 am to 6 pm in summer.
☎ *01634 402276*

4 Matfield

The Wheelwrights Arms

This is a delightful walk, gently hilly through orchards and along leafy footpaths, taking in the High Weald Landscape Trail. Matfield gets its name from a farm run by 'Matta' and the Anglo-Saxon word 'feld' meaning a large clearing. The village itself is worth exploring with its quaint pond fringed by lovely trees, its old cottages and fine houses, including the Queen Anne building, Matfield House, dating from the early 1700s. Matfield's village green is one of the largest in Kent. The First World War poet Siegfried Sassoon was born here and you can see his house 'Weirleigh' at Gedges Hill, although it is not open to the public. Sassoon's memorial stands on the green by the pond. More recently, in 1997, the village became the refuge of two daring escapees when the Tamworth Two made a bid for freedom from the slaughterhouse. The public outcry secured them a reprieve and a place of safety in Matfield, but later the sanctuary was closed down and the plucky pigs are no longer here.

THE PUB The **Wheelwrights Arms** is a white-weatherboarded, friendly Shepherd Neame pub dating from 1602. The chefs pride themselves on changing the menu frequently and offer a wide choice of food. A favourite bar snack treat is their steak baguette with fried onion, salad and chips There is home-made soup, (tomato and basil when I visited), and to follow how about lamb shank with bubble and squeak, vegetables and gravy? Vegetarians might choose baked aubergine with tomatoes, black olives and creamy sauce, for example. Smaller portions are available for children. Yummy desserts are on offer too. All the usual Shepherd Neame ales are served and there is a comprehensive wine list.

Distance – 2 miles.

OS Explorer 136 High Weald, Royal Tunbridge Wells. GR 657417

Easy footpath walking, part level, part undulating, with one 'stepped' ascent at point 4.

Starting point The Wheelwrights Arms, The Green, Matfield.

How to get there The village of Matfield lies 6 miles north-east of Royal Tunbridge Wells on the B2160. Customers are welcome to leave their cars at the Wheelwrights Arms whilst walking but please book your space by telephone as the pub can get very busy. There is additional parking around the village green.

Along the way.

Opening hours: 11 am to 11 pm on Monday to Saturday and 12 noon to 10.30 pm on Sunday. Food is served from 12 noon to 2.30 pm and 6.30 pm to 9 pm on Monday to Friday, 12 noon to 9 pm on Saturday and 12 noon to 5 pm on Sunday.
☎ *01892 722129*

With your back to the **Wheelwrights Arms**, cross the road carefully, turning left. Shortly, at **Cherry Tree Tearoom** on your right, find the signposted narrow footpath running right of the building, adjacent to a white gate. Walk between wooden fences,

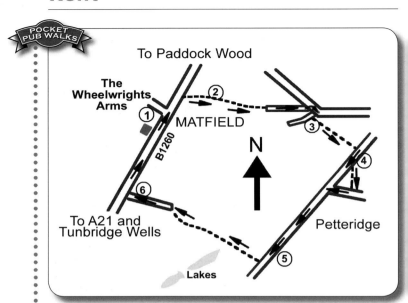

POCKET PUB WALKS

To Paddock Wood

The Wheelwrights Arms

① ②

MATFIELD

③

N

④

⑥

To A21 and Tunbridge Wells

Petteridge

⑤

Lakes

B1260

into a field. Continue ahead with the treeline on your left. After a few yards, cross a small clearing diagonally right, and continue with the new treeline to your left. The footpath curves left (signposted) and then right. Shortly, climb the stile ahead.

2 Continue ahead with a fence on your right, slightly uphill. At the opening into an orchard, follow the track to the right, with the treeline/fence on your right. Pass through the farmgate ahead (with an adjacent stile) and continue straight on past houses, turning right into a lane. Almost immediately, turn right by **Goshen Farm** and after about 10 yards, turn left onto a footpath signposted 'bridleway'.

3 After passing a house on your right, continue along the narrow footpath between fence and treeline, with orchards on your right. Begin to descend and at the end of this narrow, leafy

lane, turn right into **Petteridge Lane.** Watching for traffic, walk about 50 yards.

At a public footpath signposted left, cross carefully and enter a copse of woods, climbing steps and ascending (signposted at intervals: '**High Weald Landscape Trail**'). At the top, turn right into small cul-de-sac, then right again into the lane towards houses. (Don't avoid this part of the walk by taking the level short-cut; the alternative is a dangerous bend in Petteridge Lane.) Go past **The Hopbine** on your right, then turn left, continuing along **Petteridge Lane**.

After walking through the peaceful village of **Petteridge**, you will pass the short edge of **Porters Wood**. Take the footpath adjacent to the metal farm gate on your right, passing alongside a fencing contractor's premises, with fencing to your left and the wood to your right. Note good views over a small lake on your left as the footpath bears right. Start descending and shortly, turn right, signposted, passing the lake on your left, and continue slightly uphill.

Soon the footpath turns right and becomes a wide, tree-lined track between orchards. After passing a house on your right, climb the stile by the wooden farm gate. Turn left along the track and at the end, turn right into the road and walk the short distance back to the pub.

Places of interest nearby

The **Hop Farm Country Park**, Paddock Wood. This group of Victorian oast houses, site of a one-time working hop farm, offers family fun, with animals, museums, shire horses and play areas.
☎ *01622 872068*

5 Blue Bell Hill

The Robin Hood

Medway is steeped in history and culture and contains many well-kept areas of outstanding natural beauty. This walk offers panoramic views of meadow, farmland and woods. There are some hills to climb, but the walk is short and your efforts will be well rewarded. Blue Bell Hill, with its ancient stones and energy lines, is also famous for its crop circles. These appear frequently in a wonderful variety of formations. You can also enjoy fine views of the beautiful Weald of Kent as you walk through a part of the Burham Downs Nature Reserve.

THE PUB

The **Robin Hood**, a welcoming 14th-century, Grade II listed inn, is said to be one of the oldest in England. It was once visited by pilgrims journeying along the nearby Pilgrims' Way. Among the bar snacks there are jacket potatoes, sandwiches and baguettes, with an additional children's menu. An à la carte menu is served in the attractive restaurant and the chefs pride themselves on using fresh local produce, cooked to order. Main dishes include Dover sole and steaks. Vegetarians are also well catered for – how about the delicious mushroom stroganoff? Courage ales plus variable guest beers are available and there is a pleasant beer garden. And if that's not enough, there are also farm animals, exotic birds and a duck pond!

Opening hours are 11 am to 11 pm on Monday to Saturday and 12 noon to 10.30 pm on Sunday. Both bar and restaurant meals are served from 12 noon till 2 pm.
☎ *01634 861500*

Distance – 2 miles.

OS Explorer 148 Maidstone and the Medway Towns. GR 734628

A short, partly level, partly moderately hilly walk.

Starting point The Robin Hood in Common Road, Blue Bell Hill.

How to get there *Blue Bell Hill village is located off the A229 close to junction 3 of the M2 and is signposted (along with the crematorium). The Robin Hood is on the right about a mile along Common Road, which runs west from the village. It has a long driveway – look carefully for the signpost to the pub. Patrons may leave their vehicles in the car park whilst walking. Alternatively, you could use the car park at point 4 of the walk and start from there.*

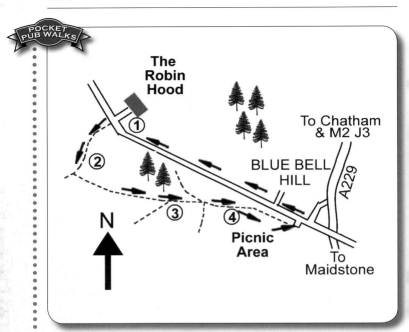

1 Leave the pub via the access road, cross **Common Road** carefully and go straight ahead down the signposted footpath on the opposite side. Continue downhill, through woods, with high banks each side. Ignore the farmgate on an incline on your left. Shortly after, you will see a signpost with a blue arrow pointing left. Follow this footpath to the left, but first enjoy the lovely views over the fence on your right.

2 After a short distance, you will reach a notice for **Burham Down Nature Reserve** on your left. Follow the yellow arrow pointing left into the reserve, passing through the kissing gate and continuing in the same direction parallel to the original footpath. There is a seat carved from a tree trunk to your right. Soon, to your right, the village of **Burham** spreads out below.

Continue until the footpath rejoins the main footpath, and start ascending. At a T-junction of footpaths, turn left.

3 Continue uphill. At the next signpost for **Burham Down Nature Reserve**, cross a bridleway and go straight ahead through a gap in the fence. Continue uphill along the footpath through woodland and go through a kissing gate on your right leading into a picnic area (signposted).

The path near the start of the walk.

Kent

4 Continue walking in the same direction as before, along the top of a steep bank, overlooking chalk quarries to your right. Pass a kissing gate on your left and ahead you will see a bench seat to rest and enjoy the superb views. Then continue to the kissing gate ahead, which leads into a small car park and viewing area. Exit the car park into **Common Road** and turn left. This is a lovely, rural road, but watch for occasional traffic. As you return to the pub enjoy the views of farmland, paddocks with horses and donkeys and meadows of wild flowers in summer.

Places of interest nearby

Kit's Coty, just to the south down the A229 (GR 745609). The remains of two prehistoric burial chambers thought to be older than Stonehenge now comprise only three upright stones, capped with a fourth large stone. Viewing is free. ☎ *01322 863467 for further details*

Aylesford Priory, to the south-west off the A229. This Carmelite friary was founded in 1242, but was subsequently dispossessed by Henry VIII. In 1949 the friars returned to restore this beautiful place to its former glory. Today it welcomes visitors who come to enjoy the sanctuary of its architecture and gardens. There are tearooms and a gift shop. ☎ *01622 717272*

The Star Inn

This is a lovely walk through the High Weald of Kent with some breathtaking views and several points of interest. These include a delightful, privately-owned, landscaped pond and a glimpse of a fine mansion, Great Maytham Hall, which is significant because the author Frances Hodgson Burnett rented it in 1898. A blocked door to the old walled garden provided her with the inspiration to write *The Secret Garden*. She left Great Maytham Hall in 1907, after which it was rebuilt.

In 1665 fire swept through Rolvenden and the population moved south to Rolvenden Layne to create a second village. All that remained of the original buildings in Rolvenden were the church and the Bull pub, once used as a court in the early 1900s where prisoners were kept in a cell in the garden. The

Distance – 2½ miles.

OS Explorer 125 Romney Marsh. GR 844313

Gentle hills; several stiles, one or two fairly high.

Starting point The Star Inn, High Street, Rolvenden.

How to get there Rolvenden is about 3 miles south-west of Tenterden on the A28. The Star is on the west side of the High Street (the A28). There is no pub car park, but ample street parking.

last recorded case was for sheep-stealing. Rolvenden today is a charming, well-kept village, with its many white-weatherboarded houses. Its lovely old church, St Mary the Virgin, was built by monks in 1220 and is said to be unchanged since 1480.

The **Star Inn** is a family pub with bars and dining facilities and an additional converted barn where you can enjoy your meal. The lovely beer garden has a delightful aspect over open fields. There is also a heated patio. The bar menu includes the local sausages, made especially in the Corker factory across the road. A delicious beef stroganoff and fresh salmon fish cakes are examples of the main dishes. The real ales are Greene King IPA, Morland Original and Abbot. This friendly pub is very popular, so it may be best to book a table.

Opening hours are 11 am to 11 pm on Monday to Saturday and 12 noon to 10.30 pm on Sunday. Food is served from 12 noon to 2.30 pm and 7 pm to 9 pm.
☎ *01580 241369*

From the **Star**, turn right into **Tenterden Road**. Cross the main road carefully, prior to reaching the bend. Turn left into **Maytham Road**, then immediately right at the signposted footpath (partially obscured by the parish board) alongside the **church of St Mary the Virgin**. Turn left, skirting the church (see the yellow arrow signposted '**High Weald Landscape Trail**).'

Look right to see a footpath leading towards a kissing gate with a wooden bench beside it. Pass through the kissing gate, also signposted '**High Weald Landscape Trail**'. Cross the field, passing through the kissing gate on the other side of the field. Bear right along a footpath. You will see, to your right, a large pond covered in water-lilies and it's worth a closer look before rejoining the main footpath. The pond is owned by a gentleman who allows no one to fish in it (except a resident heron) because the fish are 'too tame'.

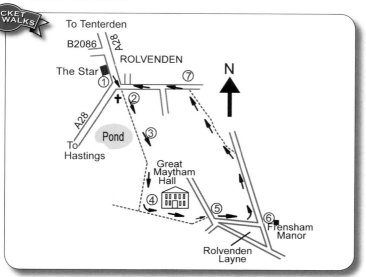

The delightful pond at point 2 of the walk.

3 After you have enjoyed the pond, continue along the footpath you were on previously, descending to the gate signposted '**High Weald Landscape Trail**'. Go through and follow the footpath between wire-linked fencing into woods, known as **The Wilderness**. Eventually, the footpath widens. At the end of the footpath, climb a stile into a meadow.

4 Turn left and almost immediately cross another waymarked stile to follow a path running along the bottom of **Great Maytham Hall**. To the left is a fine view of the house. At the end of the field, climb another waymarked stile (ignoring a stile to the right) and continue ahead with meadows to your left and stables to your right. You will reach a short, planked walkway leading to another stile. Climb the stile and follow the waymarked sign to the right, then pass through a farm gate.

5 A signpost directs you to the **High Weald Landscape Trail** across **Maytham Road**. Turn right and immediately left into **Frensham Road** at the continuation signpost. This is a lovely country lane with a footpath. At the end of the lane, you will see **Frensham Manor** opposite.

Turn left into **Winser Road**, again a quiet lane, but watch for the occasional vehicle as there is no footpath. Soon the lane ascends, with woodlands to the left. Eventually you will come to a signposted stile on your left. Climb the stile into the meadow and cross, bearing right to climb a stile fixed between wire-linked fencing and trees. Go diagonally left across the field to the opposite corner and stile. Climb the stile and turn left into **Pix's Lane**.

As you walk along **Pix's Lane**, you will see some of the finest views on this walk, as the **High Weald** spreads out into the distance on your right and undulating meadows and trees stretch to your left. Soon, ahead of you, the **Maytham Road** road sign will appear. Cross the road carefully, and turn right to walk along the raised footpath towards the church, passing **Rolvenden village hall** on your right. Turn right into **Tenterden Road** and make your way back to the pub, having enjoyed the captivating sights offered by Kent's High Weald.

Places of interest nearby

The **Motor Museum** at 63 High Street, Rolvenden, houses the C.M. Booth collection of historic vehicles, including Morgan three-wheeled cars dating from 1913.
☎ *01580 241234*

The **Kent and East Sussex Light Railway** operates steam and diesel trains through 1½ miles of delightful countryside between Tenterden in Kent and Bodiam in East Sussex. Almost all the drivers, firemen, guards and signalmen are volunteers working in their spare time.
☎ *0870 600 6074 for details of special events, timetables and fares.*

The Ringlestone Inn

Ringlestone, meaning 'ring of stones', is a tiny hamlet near Harrietsham with a fine hotel right opposite the inn. This is one of the more challenging circuits with a number of stiles, but you are rewarded with some breathtaking views across the North Downs. The entire route is on designated footpaths, although some are not too clearly defined. The walk offers a variety of farmland, woodlands and there are some hilly parts, but these should not prove too difficult.

Famous for its ghosts, the **Ringlestone Inn** is a cosy, atmospheric pub, dating from 1533, with original brick and flint walls, oak beams and inglenooks. It was once used as a hospice offering shelter to monks. During the 1960s the then landlords, a mother and daughter, became hostile towards

Distance – 4½ miles.

OS Explorer 148 Maidstone and the Medway Towns.
GR 879559

Hilly with several stiles; be prepared for patches of mud in wet weather.

Starting point The Ringlestone Inn.

How to get there Ringlestone hamlet is north of Harrietsham and 1½ miles east of the B2163 Hollingbourne to Sittingbourne road. One mile north of Hollingbourne, turn off to the south-east at the water tower and continue to Ringlestone. Customers may leave their cars at the pub while they walk but please let the landlord know before setting out.

strangers, having been intimidated by youths on motorbikes. If they disliked the look of someone, they would threaten them with a shotgun. Today's owners prefer to welcome their customers with smiles! The Ringlestone is proud of its fine selection of fruit wines – there are 31 different types. The interesting menu includes excellent home-made pies – for example, steak and ale, game, and lamb and apricot. There is also a good range of bar snacks. Shepherd Neame ales are served here and there is a large beer garden.

Opening hours: 12 noon to 3 pm and 6 pm to 11 pm on Monday to Friday, 12 noon to 11.30 pm on Saturday and 12 noon to 6 pm on Sunday. Food is served from 12 noon to 2 pm and 7 pm to 9.30 pm on Monday to Saturday and 12 noon to 2.30 pm on Sunday.
☎ *01622 859900*

Kent

1. Turn right from the **Ringlestone Inn**, then right along the side of the pub to climb the stile. Follow the waymarked footpath along a line of trees on your right, to the next stile. Climb the stile into next field, still following the treeline to your right. Eventually, the line of trees becomes woodland. When you see a long hedge facing you, bear left across the field, towards a signpost. Climb the stile by the signpost, then cross the lane (**Stede Hill**) carefully.

2. Climb the stile opposite and go along the signposted footpath through farmland, with a wire fence on your right, then a row of trees also on the right. Soon the treeline to the right disappears, and there are woods to your left. Ignoring the next left turn, follow the woodland edge, bearing left, with open fields to your right. After about 100 yards you will reach two large dead tree stumps, from which a signposted footpath runs diagonally right across the field. Aim for the stile at the end of the footpath, in the far corner. Climb this stile.

3. You are now in a quiet country lane. Cross carefully, ignoring the metalled gate almost opposite, but passing through the adjacent metal gate to its right. Follow the signposted footpath, bearing right across the field. A hand-made footpath sign is nailed on a tree to your right. Shortly, climb the stile in the middle of the facing hedgerow. From here, you will see breathtaking views across the **North Downs**. Take the footpath ahead, descending across a field, bearing slightly left. At the intersecting main track, signed '**North Downs Way**', turn left.

4. Go ahead uphill on the **Pilgrims' Way** and cross **Stede Hill** carefully. Continue along this delightful, undulating track, for about ½ mile. (Ignore two signposted stiles to conservation areas on your left.) On reaching the **Marley Road** signpost, look left for steps to a stile.

5. Climb the stile and bear right, diagonally, across the field. To your right are an enclosed field and a farmhouse. Bypass the

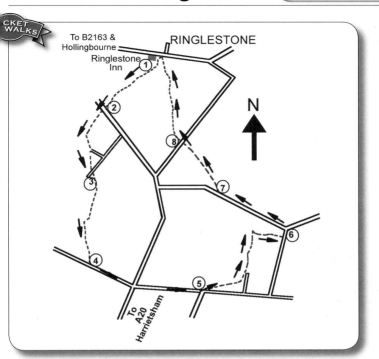

enclosed field, aiming to walk between two pylons and passing a large hillock on your left. Head for a stile in a fence between the trees facing you. Climb the stile, following the yellow arrow signposted ahead uphill. At the top of the field, turn right at the fence facing you. Walk with the fence now on your left and climb the next stile in the corner of the field. Turn left into the lane.

Ignore the first footpath left into woodlands, and walk about 30 yards along the lane before turning left into **Burchells Wood Road**. Follow this road through woodlands, ignoring the signposted footpath crossing the road. At the end of the woods, continue with open farmland on your left.

7 Turn right at the green public footpath signpost, waymarked, to another stile. Climb the stile and turn left, following yellow arrows. Continue on the footpath across wide open meadows, passing two fine oak trees which stand by the footpath ahead of you, about 70 yards apart. At the end of the footpath, climb the stile, then immediately go through a metal gate and climb slightly uphill with a hedge on your left. Climb the stile ahead and continue between hedges. Climb another stile and cross **Hogbarn Lane**.

8 Climb the opposite stile then bear diagonally right across a field, following the footpath. Climb the waymarked stile and cross the caravan park, diagonally left. Take the green public footpath sign to your right between trees. On reaching an open area, continue and climb a stile ahead into a field. Go straight ahead uphill over the brow of a field and climb the stile on the other side. Head diagonally right across this next field. Soon you will arrive at the stile you started from. Turn left to the pub for a well-earned rest after a stimulating walk.

Places of interest nearby

Leeds Castle, which is famously known as 'the loveliest castle in the world', has 500 acres of parkland with a maze, a grotto, an aviary, a vineyard and greenhouses. A must for a visit, the castle is on the A20 near Maidstone and is open daily from March till October, 10 am to 5 pm. From November to February the opening times are 10 am to 3 pm.
☎ *01622 765400*

8 Smarden Bell

The Bell

This is a beautiful walk, taking you through traditional English countryside. The sights are both delightful and interesting, with quaint cottages, oast houses, ponds and lovely views. As it is a shorter route, you should have the time and energy to enjoy looking around the nearby Wealden village of Smarden, with it pretty white-weatherboarded and half-timbered houses. Smarden became prosperous for its weaving, then, in the 19th century, hops were introduced and the oast houses in the village date from this period.

THE PUB The **Bell** was built in 1536 in the reign of Henry VIII and was once a farm dwelling and part of a large estate. Early in its history, there was also a blacksmith's forge here, then, in 1630, a cider and ale licence was granted. The Bell's original sign went up in 1769 and it became a registered hostelry. It is a cosy, welcoming pub with large open fires in winter. The food, which is home-cooked, includes traditional pub dishes such as whole-tail scampi, lasagne or beefburgers and also ciabatta with salmon and prawns or steak and onions. Main menu dishes are changed frequently for variety. Shepherd Neame ales are served and there is a comprehensive wine list. There is a beautiful garden where barbecues are held during the summer.

Opening times: lunchtimes and evenings from Monday to Thursday and all day Friday to Sunday. Food is served from 12 noon to 2.15 pm and 6.30 pm to 9.30 pm on Monday to Friday; 12 noon to 2.30 pm and 6.30 pm to 10 pm on Saturday; 12 noon to 2.45 pm and 6.30 pm to 8.30 pm on Sunday.
☎ *01233 770283*

[1] From the car park of the Bell, turn right and walk a short distance along the lane, using the grass verges where possible.

Distance – 2 miles.

OS Explorer 137 Ashford. GR 871430

Mostly level walking, but some challenging stiles. There is also an ungated railway track to cross so care should be taken.

Starting point The Bell pub in Smarden Bell.

How to get there *Smarden Bell is just north-west of the village of Smarden, to the south-east of Headcorn, off the A274. The Bell's car park is available for customers while they walk.*

Just after the junction with **Water Lane** on your right (which you ignore) turn left through a small white gate, signposted. Follow the zigzag track to the end, climb the stile and cross a footbridge into a field. Aim for the brick-built animal feeding shelter ahead, then pass a pond on your right and another on your left. Bear left, aiming for a stile just left of an outcrop of trees facing you.

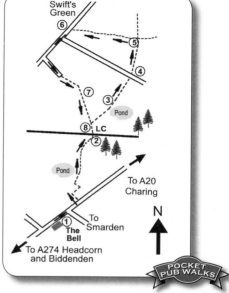

Climb this stile, then immediately climb another stile, descending steps to cross the railway line. Take extreme care, listening and looking for oncoming trains. After crossing, ascend to climb the stile on the opposite side and cross a small field to the stile ahead between the trees. Bear right, signposted on the step of the stile. Pass through the gap in the line of trees facing you, then pass a tree-lined pond in the middle of the field. The designated footpath takes you to the left of the pond.

Continue ahead to the hedgerow facing you, then turn right and climb the stile in the corner of the field by the white house and wooden pylon. Cross **Rosemary Lane** carefully, then climb the stile on the opposite side.

Walk ahead, with the hedge on your right, past a white house. Climb the stile ahead, crossing a footbridge, then almost immediately, climb another stile and cross a footbridge into a

Returning to the Bell.

field. Follow the yellow marker signposted ahead, aiming for a gap between two posts, then cross a footbridge. Bear right and climb a stile in the corner of a field, and cross the bridge over a ditch signposted ahead.

5 Keep to the right of the field for a few yards. When you reach a metal gate on your right, do not go through. Turn left and cross the open field towards the stile opposite. Climb the stile into the next field. Follow the arrow sign on the stile-step ahead, crossing the field, going over a footbridge and climbing a stile into another small field. Cross this field towards a white farmhouse with adjacent oasthouse, passing through a gap in a hedgerow next to a redundant stile. Continue to a wooden farm gate and climb the adjacent stile into **Bedlam Lane**.

Turn left along the lane. Ignore the road to the left, signposted '**Smarden**'. Shortly, turn left along a driveway signposted to **Malthouse Farm**. Pass a pond on your right, then an oast house on your left. Go straight ahead through a wooden farm gate. The short track leads through the farm and opens into a field, adjacent to a redundant stile. Cross the field to the stile ahead and climb carefully (it's poorly maintained) into the next field. Turn right.

Keep right along the edge of the field to the corner, step down into a small dip, then turn right into the next field. A line of trees runs to your left. After a few yards, find the stile on your left, climb it and go straight ahead to the railway crossing used on your outbound journey.

Climb the stile, descend steps, again cross the railway line with extreme caution, and ascend steps to the stile opposite. Immediately, climb another stile. Bear left across the field towards the animal feeding shelter, aiming for the footbridge by the white house. Cross the bridge and stile and follow the zigzag track back to the road. Turn right and retrace your steps to the pub, taking care and using the grass verges where possible. After healthy exercise, you may now enjoy some well-deserved refreshment.

Places of interest nearby

Biddenden Vineyards & Cider Works are at Little Whatmans, Gribble Bridge Lane, Biddenden, about 4 miles south-west of Smarden. The vineyards occupy a south-facing slope in a sheltered valley, beneficial to the quality of the wines. Learn about winemaking and taste some of the delicious products. Other family attractions are provided.
☎ *01580 291726*

9 Conyer Creek

The Ship Inn

This is a level walk in a figure of eight, taking you along the banks of the estuary and through meadows and orchards. The first short loop partly running alongside Conyer Creek is just a mile long, the second around 1½ miles. Conyer Creek is on the Swale estuary, a stretch of water separating the Isle of Sheppey from the mainland. This is a paradise for birdwatchers, and ducks, waders, gulls, swans, wagtails, avocets and herons are there in abundance. More recently, to the delight of locals, snowy egrets have made an appearance. Don't forget your binoculars.

THE PUB

The **Ship Inn**, (recently renamed **'The Ship and Smugglers'**), dates from 1642 and has a long nautical tradition as displayed by the memorabilia on its walls. During its colourful history, it has been a baker's and a blacksmith's, then in the early 18th century it was an alehouse and favourite haunt of smugglers. The bar food includes jacket potatoes, ploughman's and similar snacks. There is a separate restaurant – the **Smuggler** – and the main menu offers 'Doughty jumbo sausages', alongside shank of lamb with red wine and rosemary and chicken tikka. Vegetarians are catered for with 'veggie lasagne' and a delicious mushroom stroganoff. To follow, there are such delights as banoffee cheesecake or syrup sponge pudding and custard. On Sundays a traditional roast is available. If you have a strong stomach, you can eat in the 'dungeon' where there are novelty displays of skulls and skulduggery. Or climb the stairs to the 'loft sail', a charming area separate from the main restaurant, ideal for a romantic meal for two. Outside, there is a pleasant beer garden. The real ales are Adnams and Shepherd Neame's Master Brew and Spitfire.

Distance – 1, 1½ or 2½ miles.

OS Explorer 149 Sittingbourne and Faversham. GR 962648

Mostly flat, easy walking; no stiles.

Starting point The Ship Inn, The Quay, Conyer Creek.

How to get there Conyer Quay is at the head of Conyer Creek, north of Teynham, off the A2. It is 4 miles north-west of Faversham and can be reached from junction 6 of the M2. There are a few parking spaces on the Ship's property, but no proper pub car park. Street parking is available nearby.

Opening times: 6 pm to 11 pm on Monday, 11.30 am to 3 pm and 6 pm to 11 pm on Tuesday to Friday, 11.30 am to 11 pm on Saturday and 12 noon to 10.30 pm on Sunday. No food is available on Mondays, but meals and snacks are served at lunchtime during the rest of the week from 12 noon to 2 pm (3 pm on Saturday and Sunday). There are also evening meals; ring for details of times.
☎ *01795 520778*

[1] **First loop of walk:** Leave the pub garden and turn left, passing modern white-weatherboarded houses. Go through a metal kissing gate and follow the wide footpath. When the footpath divides, turn left. Continue through land once used for brickworks but now covered in low woodland.

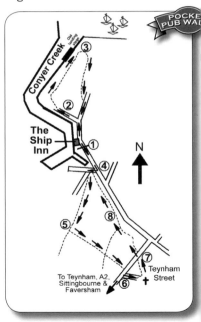

[2] Soon, the **Swale estuary** will come into view, where barges are anchored. When you see a hazard signpost (warning against slipping, so take care when muddy) turn left, downhill, along the footpath towards it. Then bear right along the raised walkway. There are views across the estuary on your left. Look out for the snowy egrets! You may also see a small island covered in wading birds. Just before you reach another hazard signpost, after passing an old landing stage, take a footpath to your right,

turning back at an acute angle.

3. Follow this path, through woodland and meadow. Look right to see the new bridge linking the mainland to the **Isle of Sheppey**. Soon, you pass a boatyard on your right. Keep straight ahead until you reach the metal

The Swale estuary.

kissing gate you passed through at the beginning of the loop and continue ahead, passing the **Ship Inn** before progressing to the second loop of your walk.

Second loop of walk: Walking to the other end of **the Quay**, turn right. Almost immediately, turn left in front of the **Swale Marina** signpost, taking the narrow footpath (signposted) through a copse of trees into a field. Keeping a hedge/treeline to your right, follow the footpath straight ahead. The masts and buildings of the marina are to your right. Keep to the footpath until you reach a crossroad of paths where you turn left. There is a playing field to the right.

Follow this fenced, tree-lined path through meadows and farmland until it meets a staggered intersection. Take the path ahead, staggered to the right, slightly uphill towards farm buildings, passing through orchards. You may see goats and donkeys in the field to your right. At the end, the track bears left into a lane. Cross carefully and go onto the wide grass verge opposite. Turn right and walk along the verge a short way towards a public footpath signposted left.

6 Turn left at this signpost, passing through a staggered metal barrier, following the fenced footpath towards a church, with a valley view to your right. Cross an intersecting track, still aiming ahead towards the church. Follow the green footpath sign to your left just before reaching the church, passing in front of farm buildings. At the end of the footpath you will reach a lane.

7 Turn right down the lane and walk for a few yards, watching carefully for traffic. To your left you will see a wide track passing a farm. Cross the road carefully and go straight ahead along this track. Shortly, turn right, waymarked. With the treeline to your right and orchards to your left, follow the footpath round two 90° turns.

8 Soon, find a gap on your right into a field. Do not pass through the gap but facing it, turn right behind the treeline and follow the footpath so that the field's fence is to your left and a ditch is to your right. Follow the fence as it curves left. Cross a wooden footbridge on your right, and then cross the field to rejoin the footpath you set out on at the beginning of the loop. Retrace your steps along the path and through the copse of trees, walking back up **the Quay** to the pub.

Places of interest nearby

Belmont Park at Throwley, 4 miles south-west of Faversham, belonged to the Harris family until the sixth Lord died in 1995 and contains fine paintings and memorabilia about the family. There are walled gardens, wooded areas and a tearoom as well as guided tours of the house. Open from April to the end of September on Saturdays, Sundays and bank holidays.
☎ 01795 890202 for details of admission and guided tours.

10 **Warehorne**

The Woolpack Inn

This is a gem of a walk through peaceful English countryside, taking in the reed-lined Royal Military Canal which runs between Hythe and Cliff End, near Hastings. It follows undulating fields and meadows, with breathtaking views from every angle. Set on a ridge, overlooking Romney Marsh, the little village of Warehorne is first mentioned in a charter of Saxon King Egbert in AD 820. The name then was 'Werehornas' which means 'a place on a bend by a weir'. Opposite the Woolpack is the lovely old church of St Matthew, the earliest part of which dates from 1200, although the nave was completed around 1450 and the tower is from the 18th century. An underground tunnel connects the pub and the church; this was built for smuggling

Distance – 2½ miles.

OS Explorer 125 Romney Marsh. GR 989325

Gentle hills and a few stiles; be prepared for some muddy patches.

Starting point The Woolpack Inn, Church Road, Warehorne.

How to get there *Warehorne is south of Ashford and just off the B2067 between Hamstreet and Woodchurch. Patrons may leave their cars in the rear car park of the Woolpack while walking. There is also street parking available.*

and extensively used. Romney Marsh, which lies south of the village, was once a haven for smugglers. On your walk, you will see a tiny church, St Mary's, Kenardington, which stands on a hill on the site of a Saxon camp. It is recorded in the Domesday Book, although originally it was probably wooden. Stormed by the Danes in AD 892, sacked by the French in the 14th century, the church was then struck by lightning and badly damaged in 1559. During Saxon times, the valley north-east of this hill would have been flooded by the sea.

THE PUB The 16th-century, white-fronted **Woolpack Inn** in the picturesque village of Warehorne is a free house, serving real ales from the cask, for example, Hopdaemon and Gadds. The interior is light and inviting, with pine tables and chairs, an open log fire in winter and a bar area strewn with hops. The lunch menu (available Tuesday to Saturday) includes a delicious meat lasagne, cod and chips, liver and bacon casserole and a home-made steakburger. Sunday lunchtime there is a choice of roasts. Ploughman's and baguettes are among the bar snacks.

The main restaurant menu offers a range of twelve dishes, including the popular steak and kidney steamed pudding, local lamb, wild rabbit or whole-tail scampi. For dessert you could tuck into chocolate lumpy bumpy or mango, passion fruit and kiwi ice cream torte. There is also a range of home-made Indian dishes. The beer garden in front of the pub is a pleasant place to eat on a sunny day.

Opening hours: Monday, 6 pm to 11 pm; Tuesday to Saturday 11.30 am to 3 pm and 6 pm to 11 pm; Sunday 12 noon to 4 pm and 7 pm to 10.30 pm. Food is served Monday 6.30 pm to 9.30 pm (no food available Monday lunchtime); Tuesday to Saturday 12 noon to 2.30 pm and 6.30 pm to 9.30 pm; Sunday 12 noon to 3 pm and 7 pm to 9 pm.
☎ *01233 733888*

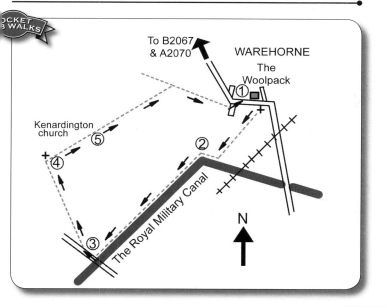

The Royal Military Canal.

1 With your back to the **Woolpack Inn**, cross the road and go into the church's main entrance. Almost immediately, to your right, climb the stile and head diagonally left across the churchyard to a stile in the corner. Climb the stile, crossing the field diagonally right, under a powerline, to the corner of the field where you pass through a gap. After a few yards, climb the stile on your left and cross the bridge on the other side. You are now at the **Royal Military Canal**.

2 Turn right, walking with the canal on your left, a small stream running parallel on your right. You will pass a Second World War bunker on your left. Glorious views spread into the distance on your right, including meadows and fields with animals grazing. Follow the lovely tree-lined canal footpath and when you pass another bunker, you will see a farmgate with an adjacent kissing gate ahead. Pass through the kissing gate into a narrow lane.

3 Turn right into the lane. After 200 yards, climb the stile signposted right and follow the footpath bearing left across the field towards the tiny church, **St Mary's, Kenardington**. Cross a stile and continue in the same direction towards the church.

4 At the church, climb the stile to the left, into the churchyard. Turn immediately right and climb the stile ahead and descend the field, ignoring a disued stile on the right. Climb the double stile ahead and continue in the same direction to climb the next stile, immediately crossing a footbridge over a stream. Cross another narrow wooden bridge. Descend steps on the other side and then cross one more bridge.

5 Keep in line with the bridge you have crossed, continuing towards a signpost. Follow the signpost diagonally left across the field to the corner. Climb a stile and continue uphill, aiming for a house with a tall chimney. Follow the footpath, passing the house to your left, aiming for the steeple of the church straight ahead. Climb a stile, walking towards the church, then pass through a metal gate. Turn left, then immediately right. It's just a short distance back to the pub and church. I hope you have enjoyed this walk, which has some of the most splendid views of any in this book.

Places of interest nearby

The **South of England Rare Breeds Centre** is a good place for families, with woodland walks, a picnic area, a restaurant and farm animals. It's located at Woodchurch, to the north-west of Warehorne via the B2067. Open all year but closed on Mondays in wintertime.
☎ *01580 715330*

The Compasses Inn

This walk is perfect for those who love wide-open spaces. Most of the route is through farmland, both crop and grazing, and a variety of magnificent views will enhance your enjoyment, for this is the English countryside at its most peaceful. Crundale and Sole Street are rather scattered communities, although the area has been a settlement for hundreds of years and is mentioned in the Domesday Book. The pub claims three ghosts, one of which is Molly Sinclair who occupies the back bar. Molly was a real person who was falsely accused of stealing eggs in the mid-1700s when the inn was a coaching house. Insisting she was innocent, she took comfort from a miller who worked nearby. Her husband found out about the affair and drowned her. It is claimed she haunts the pub in a pale blue smock and a bonnet.

Distance – 4½ miles.

OS Explorer 137 Ashford and 138 Dover, Folkestone and Hythe. GR 096493

A more challenging walk: sometimes hilly, some rough grass and muddy patches, some high stiles.

Starting point The Compasses Inn, Sole Street.

How to get there *Sole Street is off the A28 between Canterbury and Ashford. Take the turning to Crundale and Waltham, then follow the well-signposted route to Sole Street. The Compasses Inn is on your left. Customers may use the pub car park whilst walking. Alternatively, park on the verge between points 1 & 2 of the walk.*

THE PUB The lovely 15th-century **Compasses Inn** is well worth a visit, both for the warm welcome and for the fine food. There is a long cosy bar/restaurant at the front, and a delightful beer garden outside. As well as bar snacks, there's an excellent selection of main meals. Worth a special mention are the goat's cheese and caramelised onion brochettes for starters. Main courses include salmon with honey and mustard sauce or braised lamb shank in port and red wine sauce with fresh rosemary. Among the desserts is a splendid home-made banoffee pie. The real ales on offer are from Shepherd Neame.

Opening hours: 12 noon to 3 pm and 6.30 pm to 11 pm on Monday to Saturday; 12 noon to 4 pm and 6 pm to 10.30 pm on Sunday. Food is served from 12 noon to 2.30 pm and 5.30 pm to 9.30 pm on Monday to Saturday and 12 noon to 4 pm on Sunday (No food served Sunday evening).
☎ *01227 700300*

Kent

1. Turn right from the **Compasses Inn**. After approximately 300 yards, turn left at a signpost, climbing a stile adjacent to a metal gate, into a field. Go straight ahead, keeping the wire fence to your left. Continue along the tree-lined track to a metal gate and stile. Climb the stile and continue ahead with the hedgerow to your left, ignoring two gaps into the adjacent field to your left. Follow the hedgerow as it turns left at signposted markers, so you still have a hedgerow to your left and farmland to your right.

2. At the corner of the field, ignore a stile to your left and enter the field ahead. Ignore the markers on the signpost to the left and those pointing diagonally across the field. Instead, turn right along a wide grass track. You will now be skirting the right outside perimeter of a field, which opens up into an even larger field.

3. Continue following the outside perimeter of the field as it bends and curves. Keep the hedgerow/treeline to your right. There will be fine views into a valley to your right and a farmhouse spread out below. When you see farm buildings ahead of you, follow the track, climbing a low hill towards the farm.

4. At the wire fence facing you, turn left, so it is now to your right with farm buildings behind it. Turn right at the corner most of the wire fence. Do not go through the metal gate ahead of you. Follow the yellow arrow signposted left. A short way the farm, a yellow arrow directs you to the right through a smaller metal gate. Follow the fenced track between small fields. Pass through the wooden gate at the end onto a single-track tarmac lane.

5. Cross the lane and pass through another wooden gate. Cross the meadow straight ahead and enter the wood through another small metal gate signposted ahead. Follow the footpath through woods, gradually descending. When a track crosses your path, follow the yellow arrow signposted left. At the edge of the wood, another yellow arrow directs you ahead, taking you

ERRATUM SLIP
SOLE STREET WALK

It has been necessary to slightly shorten and amend this walk, but the directions below will take you to point ⑥ line 8 on the opposite page 'Just before reaching the corner of the field …' From this point, please continue with the book directions to the end of the walk.

1 Turn right with your back to the **Compasses Inn**. After approximately 300 yards, turn left, climbing a stile adjacent to a metal gate, into a field. Go straight ahead, keeping the wire fence to your left. Continue along the tree-lined track to a metal gate and stile. Climb the stile and continue ahead with the hedgerow on your left.

2 Follow the hedgerow and on reaching a waymarked junction with a bridleway, turn left and walk along the field edge to the next corner.

3 Cross into the field in front of you and go diagonally right, following the waymarked path across the field to the far side. Continue on the bridleway, keeping the hedgerow on the left.

4 Soon you reach the road (Woods Hill) opposite the turning to **Grandacre Farm**. Turn right and follow the lane, passing the entrance to **Ashenfield Farm**.

5 Where a right of way crosses the road by a corrugated iron hut, turn left and continue along the edge of the field, with the hedgerow on your left.

You are now at point ⑥, line 8, on the opposite page.

slightly diagonally right across a field. Aim for a gap between trees alongside a corrugated iron hut and onto a lane (**Woods Hill**).

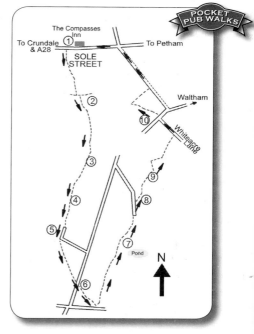

POCKET PUB WALKS

The Compasses Inn

To Crundale & A28

SOLE STREET

To Petham

Waltham

Whiteacre Lane

Pond

N

5] Turn right into the lane, then cross the road and turn immediately left, following the signpost-ed footpath. Continue along the edge of the field, with the hedgerow on your left. Just before reaching the corner of the field, turn left at the blue arrow signposted into a field, keeping to the right edge along-side trees. Still keeping woodland to your right, follow the track ahead, soon curving to the left and passing a pond on your right.

7] Turn right at the blue arrow posted on a pylon and go along a fenced track. At the end of the track, pass through a wooden farm gate, following the arrow pointing diagonally left across a meadow and passing through the metal farm gate opposite. Continue between house and farm buildings, walking a short way along a tarmac road. At the point where a notice bans further progress, turn right through a gate between blue-banded posts into a field.

8] Bear left, aiming for another metal gate with a blue-banded post at the far end of the field. Pass through this gate and walk along the right edge of the next field. Ignore a minor footpath to

Kent

your right entering woods. Go through the gate ahead into the next field. Begin descending, now with woodland to your right. Follow the treeline as it turns abruptly right and you will see a wooden gate ahead with a blue-banded post. Go through the gate and take the left fork of the bridleway, indicated by a blue arrow on a tall post cornering a fenced field.

9 Follow the bridleway round two 90° bends, then climb the ridge ahead, leaving the fenced field behind you. Turn right along the ridge, passing a disused farm building on your left, and follow the footpath ahead through woods. Pass through the metal gate ahead, keeping a high wire fence to your right. To your left is the rear of a house. Turn left through a metal gate onto a lane.

10 Turn left uphill (**Whiteacre Lane**). At the T-junction, cross the road carefully and climb a high stile slightly staggered to your right, into a field. Go straight ahead across the field and climb two stiles close together. Cross the next field, bearing right towards a footpath between the trees in the corner. This footpath runs between houses, exiting onto **Richdore Road**. Turn left and continue along the road till you reach a crossroads. Turn left and the pub is a short way along on the right.

Places of interest nearby

Why not travel south of Sole Street to Wye and visit the **Wye National Nature Reserve**, just south-east of Wye. It is managed by the Wye Campus of Imperial College, London, and designated a Site of Special Scientific Interest. See if you can find some of the nineteen species of orchids that grow there (three of them very rare). The reserve has waymarked trails.
☎ *01233 812525*

12 **Blean**

The Hare and Hounds

This is a pleasant, easy walk, mostly on well-laid tracks and footpaths through a variety of open and wooded landscapes. The ancient forest of Blean was once used by royalty for hunting and later became a haunt of smugglers. At one time it stretched from the Great Stour, to the east of Canterbury, to the coast. Blean Woods is now a nature reserve and is teeming with protected plants and animals. The village of Blean comprises a few houses on a hill, and on this delightfully picturesque walk you will pass its interesting 13th-century church, St Cosmus and St Damian-in-the-Blean, notable for its ancient architectural beauty. Somewhere in the churchyard is the unmarked grave of Agnes Gibbs, who died at two years old in 1851, and was only 18 inches tall. She was born at Luckett's Farm in Blean and caught the attention of the Duchess of Kent, who had her examined by her physicians. The child was said to be perfectly formed in miniature. Her father was the local vicar, and he had her buried in the unmarked grave to avoid being targeted by grave-robbers.

THE PUB The excellent, spacious **Hare and Hounds** provides a variety of bar snacks and main meals, and next door is an Italian restaurant that is also run by the publican, with the maxim: 'Eat Italian, live longer, eat at Angelo's, live forever!' Most people need no introduction to the pleasures of Italian food, but there is more to the Mediterranean cuisine served here than pizzas and pasta. Angelo's menu offers a range of delicious, authentic Italian meals, including tasty vegetarian dishes, so there is something to suit everyone – from the no-nonsense but delicious minestrone soup to the more exotic king prawns in a wine and garlic sauce. And if that isn't enough – well, full English breakfasts are served in the pub from 8.30 am daily. There is also a beer garden.

Distance – 5 miles.

OS Explorer 150 Canterbury and the Isle of Thanet. GR 126604

A partly level, partly hilly walk through farmland and woods.

Starting point The Hare and Hounds in Blean.

How to get there The village of Blean is situated 3 miles north-west of the centre of Canterbury on the A290. The pub is on Blean Hill, on your right if approaching from Canterbury. Customers may use the car park whilst walking.

POCKET
PUB WALKS

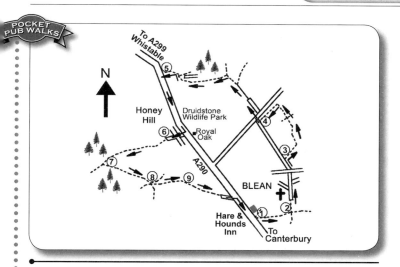

Opening hours: 8.30 am till midnight, seven days a week. Food (breakfast) served from 8.30 am.
☎ *01227 471594*

1 From the **Hare and Hounds**, turn left and cross the extended car park diagonally left, passing through a signposted gap in the trees in the far corner. Go through a kissing gate and take the footpath forked to the right. A stream runs on your right. Soon, climb the stile, signposted ahead, into a meadow, and continue with woodlands on your right. Turn left along a tarmac track crossing your path (a bridge crossing the stream is on your right).

2 Continue along the track, slightly ascending, enjoying the open countryside. Pass the **church of St Cosmus and St Damian-in-the-Blean**. Soon, look right at the gardens of **Church Cottage**, with its large lily-pond. Carefully cross **Tyler Hill Road** and go straight ahead, passing stables on your right. Just before you reach a wooden cyclists' gateway, turn right along a signed footpath.

3 Hedgerows and fields line each side of the footpath. At one point the right hedgerow peters out, then reappears, but keep to the path. The footpath opens out into a large apple orchard, to your right. Continue for about 50 yards, then turn left onto a signposted footpath between two hedgerows. Follow this footpath through an open farm gate, overhung by willows, towards greenhouses ahead of you. On reaching the greenhouses, turn immediately right, with caravans, greenhouses and farm buildings to your left.

4 Continue along this footpath, carefully cross **Chapel Lane** and go straight ahead along the footpath signposted to **Clowes Wood** and **Whitstable**. Pass a farm on your right and open countryside on your left. Ignore a stile on your left and, a little further, ignore the public footpath signposted right. Keep to the path through farmland till you reach a pine wood. Take the first footpath, signposted left, leading into the woods downhill. Eventually, the path levels out. At a redundant stile to your left, turn left through the large gap beside it and follow the footpath to the end.

5 At an opening into a field, keep to the right hedgerow. At the farmgate ahead, pass through the adjacent gap into **Honey Hill** and turn left. Start ascending, passing **Meadow Grange Nursery** on your left and **Druidstone Wildlife Park**, also on your left. Just before the **Royal Oak pub** on your left, look right for a signposted cul-de-sac into **Woodlands Estate**. It is dangerous to cross the road here: instead, go past the **Royal Oak** to cross at the traffic island, and double back to **Woodlands Estate**, now on your left.

6 Follow the road into **Woodlands Estate** as it curves right, then bear left and straight ahead between park homes, downhill, towards **Blean Nature Reserve**. At the farm gate, pass through the adjacent gap and continue ahead along the undulating footpath. Ignore minor, unsignposted footpaths left through woods. Keep to the curving main path, passing through old gateposts. The woods thin out on your right, revealing lovely views.

At an intersection of footpaths, where the woods thicken, turn left, following the yellow arrow on a post, slightly uphill, eventually reaching a large clearing.

Bear left, following the curved footpath across the clearing, signposted by a black arrow. At the far corner, follow the black arrow signposted ahead, crossing the intersecting track, and continue straight ahead along the signposted woodland footpath. At a fork, turn right, following the black arrow. After about 200 yards, ignore the black arrow signposted ahead, and turn left along a footpath. Soon, cross a main track and continue ahead. On reaching an **English Nature** signpost (facing you) turn left and follow the footpath to a metal kissing gate.

Go through the gate, cross the field diagonally right and climb a stile. Cross the next field to climb a stile almost opposite, set slightly left. Turn left along a footpath, tree-lined and fenced both sides. On reaching the bottom of a cul-de-sac, follow it to the road. Cross the road safely to use the footpath opposite, turning right. It is a short distance back to the pub and some well-deserved refreshment after a stimulating walk.

Places of interest nearby

The **Druidstone Wildlife Park** in Honey Hill passed at point 5 of the walk is famous for its natural beauty. It provides a sanctuary for sick or injured animals and there is a farmyard and a trail through an 'Enchanted Wood' with a sleeping dragon and other magical creatures – ideal for children! A pond is home to a variety of waterfowl, including black swans. Late spring is an especially good time to visit when the bluebells are on display.
☎ *01227 765168*

13 Paddlesworth

The Cat and Custard Pot

Paddlesworth is on the North Downs. This is a beautiful, undulating walk through hills and pasture, with glorious views but no steep ascents. If you enjoy looking at animals and birds, you will be in for a treat; besides plenty of black-faced sheep and inquisitive horses, you might be lucky enough to spot game birds, peacocks, yellow-hammers, green woodpeckers and even a hare racing across the fields. The grass footpath on the return journey is especially charming, with fine views to left and right. You will walk short distances along quiet country lanes, but these are equally appealing, offering plenty of sights to enjoy.

THE PUB Once, the Cat and Custard Pot was known as the Red Lion. When the signboard blew down, a new board was designed by the village artist. This lion had pricked ears and whiskers and the pub was renamed 'The Cat'. Then it became the Cat and

Mustard Pot and now it's the Cat and Custard Pot. It used to be frequented by pilots and other personnel stationed at the nearby Hawkinge Battle of Britain airfield and it displays some interesting aviation memorabilia. The scrumptious menu includes all our old favourites, rump steak and breaded mushrooms, butterfly chicken breast with garlic butter and chilli con carne, as well as lighter snacks like jackets, sandwiches and ploughman's. There are also vegetarian options such as a tasty home-made curry. The pub serves traditional ales such as Master Brew and Spitfire. However, take some real money with you – they do not accept credit or debit cards.

Opening hours: 12 noon to 3 pm and 7 pm to 11 pm (10.30 pm on Sunday, Monday and Tuesday). Food is served from 12 noon to 2 pm and 7 pm to 9 pm but please note no food is available on Sunday evening.
☎ *01303 892205*

Distance – *2 miles.*

OS Explorer 138 Dover, Folkestone and Hythe. GR 195398

Occasionally hilly, with a few stiles, but comfortable walking.

Starting point The Cat and Custard Pot in Paddlesworth.

How to get there *Paddlesworth is just outside the village of Hawkinge, around 15 minutes' drive from Folkestone, reached via the A260. Take Aerodrome Road off the A260, and follow signs to Paddlesworth. The Cat and Custard Pot has a large car park, where customers may leave their vehicles whilst walking.*

1 Turn left out of the **Cat and Custard Pot** car park and follow the bend curving right. After 50 yards, take a track to your left through farmland, shortly passing a yellow-arrowed signpost. Climb a stile beside a metal gate, and immediately climb a second stile. Cross the field to the stile straight ahead and climb it, signposted ahead to another stile. Climb this stile into a copse, passing a pond to your right. A single-track tarmac road crosses your path.

2 Cross the tarmac road, bearing slightly right. Ignore the first left gap into a field. Pass through the metal gate, uphill, where the footpath is signposted with a yellow-banded post behind a large tree (ignore the adjacent gate far right). Continue ahead with a hedge to your left until a farm track crosses your path, with farm buildings to the right.

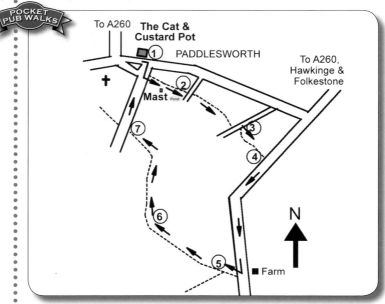

One of the many fine views to be enjoyed.

Turn left along this track for a few yards, then right into an open field, alongside a hedgerow, to your right. At the end of the hedgerow, the field opens out. Cross it diagonally to your left (designated footpath), making for the far corner. The signpost and exit-gap between the trees is slightly to the right of this far corner.

Pass through the gap onto **Elvington Lane** and turn right, uphill, watching for occasional vehicles. Pass a Second World War fortification to your left, then farm buildings. Start descending, soon passing **Airgrove House** on your left. On reaching **Dane Farm** on your left, immediately turn right along the signposted public bridleway opposite. As you reach the metal gate, do not pass through but bear right along a blue-arrow signposted footpath.

5 Continue along the leafy footpath, with views on either side. Soon you will pass through a metal gate, bearing right, following another blue-arrow sign. Bear left at an intersection and go through another metal gate, signposted with a blue arrow. After approximately 200 yards, pass through yet another metal gate and continue uphill, following the winding footpath. Look behind you at lovely views. Pass through one more metal gate, and almost immediately climb a stile.

6 Continue along the footpath, which now descends. You will reach a wire-fenced game bird enclosure ahead. Don't trip over a wire extending a short way at a right-angle from the fence. Turn right, skirting the enclosure, which curves left and descends to a small stile. Just before the stile, watch out for another extended wire. Climb the stile and cross the field diagonally left to the far corner. In the adjacent field there is a Second World War pillbox. Go through the metal gate into this adjacent field, passing the pillbox.

7 Turn left to exit the field through another metal gate onto the unnamed lane running from **Arpinge** to **Paddlesworth**. Turn right and continue slightly uphill, then descend. Watching for occasional traffic, follow this lane back to the pub.

Places of interest nearby

The **Battle of Britain Museum** in Aerodrome Road, Hawkinge has an interesting collection of artefacts, including aircraft and a variety of relics from the period. It has a shop, snacks and free parking. Open from Good Friday till the end of September, Tuesday to Sunday, 10 am to 5 pm (closed on Mondays except bank holidays).
☎ *01303 893140*

14 St Nicholas at Wade

The Bell Inn

T**hanet is a paradise** for wild flowers, reeds and grasses, and an important refuge for butterflies and birds of marshland and coast. The flat terrain provides for comfortable walking and big beautiful skies, which were much admired by artist J.M.W. Turner, who came to Thanet to paint them. The coastal part of the walk runs between the sea and the marshlands, an ideal combination for naturalists. The seawall was completed around 1808 but was badly breached by a storm in 1953. It is still being strengthened and contains many fossils. Depending on season, you may see swallows and swifts in their crazy, dipping flight as they snap up insects on the wing, as well as wagtails, warblers and waders. Cormorants are a familiar sight, taking up

Kent

Distance – 5 miles.

OS Explorer 150 Canterbury and the Isle of Thanet. GR 266666

Mostly flat, easy walking.

Starting point The Bell Inn, The Street, St Nicholas at Wade on the Isle of Thanet.

How to get there From the A299 Thanet Way between Herne Bay and the A28 south-west of Margate, turn off for St Nicholas at Wade. The Bell Inn is near the church. Customers may use the pub car park while walking, but please be sure to seek permission first.

residence on the marker poles to fish and holding their wings out to dry. Take care not to disturb swans at rest among the reeds in the marshes, especially if they have cygnets.

THE PUB One of Thanet's oldest pubs, the **Bell Inn** dates back to 1622 when it was run by William Chambers, who was censured by the church for tippling and drinking! In spite of a modern frontage, its Tudor heritage is still in evidence. There is a main bar and separate restaurant, which specialises in seafood. If you wish to sample the seafood platter, please telephone in advance as it's a special dish and they need notice. There is also an à la carte menu which includes pan-fried Thai chilli king prawns and fresh skate in black butter. Desserts include crème brulée, profiteroles and cheesecake. The beers include draught Bass and Flowers IPA. A point of interest in the main bar is a fine ducks' nest fireplace, so called because of the shape of the grate. Also note the uneven floor in this atmospheric old pub. Outside there is a large beer garden.

Opening hours: 12 noon to midnight on Sunday to Thursday and 12 noon to 1 am on Friday and Saturday (please note that they close after lunch on Monday to Thursday from 3 pm to 5 pm). Food is served from 12 noon daily.
☎ *01843 847250*

As you leave the **Bell Inn**, turn left, towards **St Nicholas' church**. Watch for traffic here, as there is no footpath. Worth noting is a tiny building, **The Farriers' Cottage** on your left, opposite the church, dating from the early 1600s. Turn right just past the church into **Shuart Lane**, passing **The Granary** on your left. This lane contains some fascinating buildings including the 16th-century **Cherry Tree Cottage** on your left. Cross the ramped footbridge over **Thanet Way** dual carriageway and enjoy panoramic views over **Thanet**.

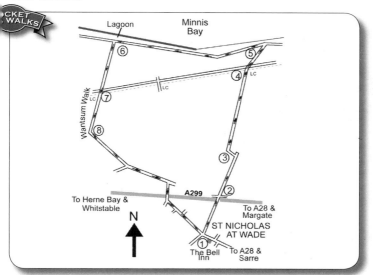

2 On leaving the footbridge, carefully cross **Potten Street Road** and continue along **Shuart Lane,** past the **Hedgend Industrial Estate**. On a clear day, you will see the twin towers of **Reculver** on your left, the remains of an ancient abbey. When you reach the remains of a barn on your right, you will see ahead an intersection of paths. A signpost indicates a bridleway ahead and a footpath to the left. Take the footpath left.

3 As you walk along the footpath, look right to see a lovely old house standing on **Shuart Farm**, built in the Dutch style. During Elizabethan times the Dutch came to drain the Thanet marshes and this house is their legacy. Adjacent is a granary raised up on stilts to prevent mice and rats from climbing in to get at the grain. Go straight ahead, onto the **Wantsum Walk**, a farm track edged with hedgerows. Eventually, the hedgerow peters out and the vista opens up to a high ridge ahead. There's a small stream to your right.

4 On reaching the ridge, cross the gated level crossing with care. Then continue, bearing right along the track until you reach the seawall, go up the seven steps and you are at **Minnis Bay**.

5 Turn left along the seawall and towards the **Reculver towers** visible ahead of you. The seawall divides the coastline and marshes, presenting two beautiful aspects. The area to your left is known as **Plum Pudding Island**. If you look to your left, you'll see St **Nicholas' church tower** on the skyline and pass a saltwater lagoon on your right. After you have walked along the seawall for about one mile, the path changes colour from a dark tarmac to a light sandy pink and you will be by another saltwater lagoon.

6 About two-thirds of the way along the lagoon, turn left at a signpost to '**Pegwell Bay**'. *(You could continue straight ahead to take a look at the Reculver towers and backtrack to this point for the return journey. This would add an extra 3 miles there and back.)* Now

St Nicholas at Wade

you are walking along the **Wantsum Walk** farm track – this is real Thanet marshland. When you reach the ridge, turn left at the '**Viking Coastal Trail**' sign, walk uphill a few yards, and then turn right at the next '**Viking**' signpost, to a gated level crossing.

Again, cross with care. Now you have a choice: either (a) continue along the farm track or (b) turn immediately right towards the stream (and on reaching the stream, bear left and follow the parallel path). The latter option is recommended, especially if you like to see swans basking their snowy feathers in the sunshine. Whichever path you choose, farm track or stream footpath, you'll arrive at the **Wantsum Angling Association** car park. Continue ahead till you come to a field.

Do not enter the field. Turn left, signposted, following a concrete track. Pass farm buildings and continue up **Potten Street**. Turn right to cross a road/footbridge over the **Thanet Way** and continue ahead to the church. Once again, take care here as there is no footpath. Before long you will be back at the **Bell Inn**, ready to enjoy its cosy ambience and a refreshing drink

Places of interest nearby

Sarre Windmill, which is just over a mile south of St Nicholas at Wade, dates from around 1820. Its pleasant teashop/café also contains a marvellous healthfood shop full of tasty produce from cereals to free-range eggs and organic biscuits and honey. There is a small charge to look around this interesting working mill, said to be haunted by the friendly ghost of a former miller. The land behind the mill was once an ancient Saxon burial ground. Open every day during school holidays, otherwise Tuesday to Sunday, 10 am to 5 pm.
☎ *01843 847573*

The Three Compasses

If you enjoy seaside walks, this is the one for you, as it follows the Saxon Shore Way along a lovely stretch of coastline. Although a port, there was never a harbour or dock at Deal. A naturally sheltered part of the sea is bounded by sandbanks; the notorious Goodwin Sands, which lie 3½ miles off the Deal seashore, protecting anchored ships. This protection sometimes aided rescue for foundering ships, but, sadly, shipwrecked crews

Distance – 5½ miles.

OS Explorer 150 Canterbury and the Isle of Thanet. GR 377530

Easy level walking; a short distance on a shingle path.

Starting point The Three Compasses, Beach Street, Deal.

How to get there Deal is 8 miles north-east of Dover on the A258. Turn left along the seafront and find the Three Compasses on your left on the corner of Coppin Street. There is plenty of public car parking and promenade parking close to the pub.

and passengers were frequently plundered by the locals. Daniel Defoe, author of *Robinson Crusoe*, penned the following words: 'The barbarous, hated name of Deal should die or be a term of infamy.' Today, the town of Deal is both quaint and surprising. On your walk you can see the house where Big Chief I-Spy lived. During the 1950s and 1960s, I-Spy books were popular spotter guides for children on various subjects: birds, cars, planes, etc. Children recorded seeing the items and then sent their completed book to the self-appointed Red Indian Chief who awarded them a 'redskin' feather. This was the antiques dealer Arnold Cawthrow. On the return route you will be using the Ancient Highway that runs from Sandwich to Deal for part of the way. This is a charming rural road with open view of golf links, countryside and farmland.

The **Three Compasses** is a Grade II listed building with a light, modern interior in the Continental style and is well worth a visit. The menu – always tempting – is changed frequently, and all the food is made on the premises, including the delicious bread: black olive, poppy seed and walnut. Hand pumped beers are changed weekly and one or two special ales are available such as Warsteiner and a wheat beer called Erdinger.

Opening hours: 7 pm to 11 pm on Wednesday and Thursday; 12 noon to 5 pm and 7 pm to 11 pm on Friday and Saturday; 12 noon to 5 pm on Sunday. Food is served until an hour before closing. If you are here at a time when the Three Compasses is not open, you will find plenty of other good pubs nearby.
☎ *01304 374661*

1 Turn left out of the **Three Compasses** and walk along the pavement. About 70 yards along on your left, you will see a building with two plaques on the front. This was the home

Horseriders on the route

of Arnold Cawthrow, Big Chief I-Spy. After looking at the house, cross the road and continue walking in the same direction along the seawall for about ½ mile, to the end.

Climb the steps at the end of the seawall walk. Ignoring the signpost ahead of you, turn right onto a wide shingle path following the coastline. (Shortly, the shingle disperses, making walking more comfortable.) To your left are the slopes of the golf course. Follow this coastal footpath. Pass and ignore a left signpost to the **Chequers** on your left, and continue straight ahead towards buildings.

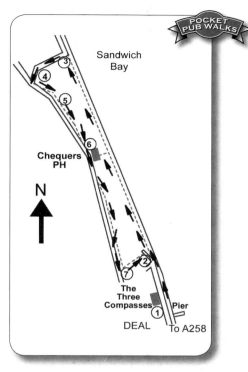

When you pass the **Sandwich Bay Sailing and Water Ski Club** on your left, go through a kissing gate ahead and turn left along the side of the building. Go through a gap beside the metal gate ahead, onto a track. Follow the track, between wire fencing, for a short way, passing a small boatyard.

At the end of the track, climb a stile onto the 'Ancient Highway' **Deal** to **Sandwich** road. Turn left into the road and almost immediately follow a track forking left off the Ancient Highway.

Kent

A fence runs to your left. After about 100 yards, where the track bends back at an acute angle, bear right onto another track, towards an old 'Private Property' signpost.

5. The public footpath is marked out by white marker posts and runs parallel with the Ancient Highway. Walk between these white posts through the golf links. When the track rejoins the Ancient Highway, turn left. This is a quiet toll road but watch for occasional traffic.

6. Follow the road as it curves left past the **Chequers Restaurant**, with a barn to your right. After about 70 yards, turn left through a gap in the long grass onto a low footpath, turning right to continue in the same direction towards **Deal**. Soon, the footpath rejoins the road and there are some white buildings ahead.

7. A short distance past the buildings, you will reach a **National Cycle Network** milepost on your left. Turn left, in front of houses, and walk along the edge of the golf course or on the alternative public footpath behind hedges, towards the seawall. Retrace your steps back to **Deal seafront** along the seawall, to enjoy a few more bracing ocean breezes before welcome refreshment.

Places of interest nearby

Once, **Richborough Castle** stood on the coast and it was the bridgehead from which the Romans began their invasion in AD 43. A monumental archway was built to mark the conquest of Britain and evidence of its foundations still exists, as well as the remains of the massive fortified wall and defensive ditches. There is also a museum. The castle is located 2 miles north of Sandwich off the A256, and is open daily from April to November.
☎ *01304 612013*